Guid FIWARE

Practical Guide

A. De Quattro

Guide to FIWARE

1.Introduction to FIWARE

FIWARE is an open source, industry-standard platform aimed at accelerating the development of smart and innovative solutions for smart cities and the Internet of Things (IoT). Introduced in 2011 by the European Union as part of the Horizon 2020 research and innovation program, FIWARE offers a range of tools, components, and open standards that allow developers to easily create interoperable and scalable applications and services.

One of the main goals of FIWARE is to foster the creation of an open and decentralized digital ecosystem, where data and services can be securely and transparently shared among different organizations, sectors, and countries. This platform-as-a-service (PaaS) approach allows developers to focus on creating added value for end users, without having to worry about the underlying complexity of the technological infrastructure.

FIWARE is designed to support a wide range of sectors and use cases, including smart transportation, sustainable energy, tourism, agriculture, healthcare, and industry. The platform provides advanced tools for real-time data management, security, interoperability, and scalability, enabling developers to quickly prototype, test, and deploy new digital solutions.

Key components of FIWARE include the Orion Context Broker, a middleware for real-time contextual data management; IoT Agent, for interfacing with IoT devices and sensors; WireCloud, a visual development environment for creating dashboards and web applications; and IDAS, for collecting, processing, and storing data from connected devices.

Additionally, FIWARE supports open and interoperable standards such as OMA

LWM2M for IoT device management, MQTT for publish/subscribe communication, and NGSI for contextual data modeling. Thanks to this modular and flexible architecture, developers can easily integrate new components and services into the platform, customizing it to their needs and requirements.

Another significant advantage of FIWARE is its cloud-based nature, which allows developers to deploy their applications in a scalable and reliable manner, without having to worry about managing the underlying infrastructure. This approach reduces development and management costs, allowing organizations to focus on their core competencies and accelerate the time-to-market of their solutions.

FIWARE has quickly gained global popularity, becoming one of the preferred platforms for startups, businesses, and public entities to develop smart and innovative solutions. Additionally, the FIWARE community is active and dynamic, providing support to new developers, organizing events and workshops, and contributing to the continuous improvement of the platform.

FIWARE represents a unique opportunity for developers to harness the power of digital technologies to create innovative and sustainable solutions for the challenges of the future. With its open, modular, and interoperable architecture, FIWARE offers an ideal environment for collaboration and innovation, allowing developers to realize the full potential of digitization and IoT.

2.FIWARE Architecture

Fiware is an open-source platform that offers a range of tools and components for the development and management of smart IoT (Internet of Things) and smart city applications. The architecture of Fiware is designed to be flexible, scalable, and interoperable, allowing developers to easily create innovative solutions for a wide range of sectors, such as health, energy, transportation, and more.

The Fiware architecture is based on a series of core components that work together to enable applications to access and manage a vast amount of real-time data from IoT devices. These components include:

- FIWARE Context Broker: This component manages the business logic between applications and sensor data, allowing applications to access information about objects (such as people, buildings, vehicles, etc.) in real-time. The Context Broker stores this information in a standard format called NGSI (Next Generation Service Interface) and makes it available to applications through RESTful APIs.

- FIWARE IoT Agent: This component is responsible for communicating with IoT devices and transmitting data to the Context Broker. The IoT Agent supports a wide range of communication protocols, such as MQTT, CoAP, and HTTP, making it easy to connect any type of IoT device to the Fiware platform.

- FIWARE Data Handling: This component manages the incoming data from the Context Broker and the IoT Agent. It handles data storage, processing, and analysis, allowing for the generation of valuable insights for application optimization.

- FIWARE Identity Manager: This component manages user identity and provides authentication and authorization functionalities. It allows developers to define roles and permissions to access platform resources and ensure data security.

- FIWARE Data Marketplace: This component allows users to share and monetize data generated by sensors. Developers can create data and service offers in the marketplace and earn revenue by selling these offers to other businesses or users.

- FIWARE Security: The Fiware architecture also includes a set of tools and protocols to ensure data security and user privacy, such as end-to-end encryption, two-factor authentication, and access monitoring.

These components are designed to be modular and interoperable, allowing developers to easily customize and integrate new features into the Fiware platform. Additionally, Fiware offers a wide range of tools and APIs to facilitate the rapid development of smart applications and the creation of interconnected solution ecosystems.

Another important aspect of the Fiware architecture is its ability to horizontally scale to handle large volumes of real-time data. Node clusters can be easily added or removed to adapt to load requirements and ensure reliable and fast performance.

The Fiware architecture provides a solid foundation for the development of smart IoT and smart city solutions, enabling developers to quickly create scalable and innovative applications. With its flexibility, interoperability, and security, Fiware stands out as a reference platform for creating intelligent service and solution ecosystems for the future.

3.Main components of FIWARE

FIWARE is an open-source platform that provides a set of tools and technologies for the development of smart city, IoT, and industrial solutions. Its main components are diverse and cover a wide range of functionalities, from data management to security, scalability to legacy systems integration. In this article, we will analyze in detail the main components of FIWARE and their characteristics.

1. FIWARE Orion Context Broker: One of the key components of FIWARE is the Context Broker, a middleware that manages and organizes data from various sources into a single context. This allows applications to easily access real-time data and information, facilitating the development of intelligent and responsive solutions. The Context Broker supports various communication protocols such as MQTT, CoAP, and HTTP, and also offers functionalities for data filtering, aggregation, and subscription.

2. FIWARE Data Management: Another fundamental component of FIWARE is Data Management, which provides tools for managing, storing, and analyzing data from sensors, devices, and other sources. This component includes modules for data ingestion, transformation, and processing, as well as for creating distributed databases and managing access and security policies.

3. FIWARE Identity Management: Security is a critical aspect for IoT and smart city solutions, and FIWARE offers an Identity Management module to ensure secure access to data and resources. This component allows for managing user and device identities, authenticating and authorizing accesses, and implementing customized security policies to protect sensitive data.

4. FIWARE Application Framework: For the development of intelligent and innovative

applications, FIWARE provides an Application Framework that includes tools and libraries for creating intuitive user interfaces, data and resource management, application scalability, and distribution. This component supports various development technologies such as Node.js, Java, and Python, and also offers a plugin and extension ecosystem to extend basic functionalities.

5. FIWARE IoT Agent: To easily integrate IoT devices and sensors into the FIWARE platform, an IoT Agent module is available that provides a standardized interface for device communication and management. This component supports various communication protocols such as MQTT, CoAP, and HTTP, and offers functionalities for device discovery, registration, and remote control.

6. FIWARE Monetization: To monetize smart city and IoT solutions based on FIWARE, a Monetization module is available to manage payments, rates, and transactions related to the

use of applications and services. This component supports various payment methods such as credit cards, bank transfers, and cryptocurrencies, and offers functionalities for reporting, monitoring, and analyzing transactions.

7. FIWARE Marketplace: Lastly, to foster collaboration among developers, providers, and users of FIWARE-based solutions, a Marketplace is available as a meeting point for sharing applications, services, and resources. This component offers tools for research, evaluation, and purchase of solutions, as well as for publishing and promoting products and services based on FIWARE.

In summary, the main components of FIWARE cover a wide range of functionalities for the development of smart city, IoT, and industrial solutions, providing tools and technologies for data management, security, device integration, application development, and monetization. Thanks to these components, FIWARE stands as a comprehensive and flexible platform for the innovation and digitization of urban services and infrastructures.

4. FIWARE Orion Context Broker

FIWARE Orion Context Broker is an open-source software component developed by FIWARE, a global community focused on building an open-source ecosystem for the development of intelligent applications and services based on real-time data. Orion Context Broker is a key tool in the FIWARE platform, as it manages and provides real-time context information required for intelligent and responsive applications.

The Context Broker is designed to handle real-time data from a variety of sources, such as IoT sensors, monitoring systems, and connected devices. This data is organized into entities and attributes, which represent objects and their properties in the context of applications. For example, an entity could be a temperature sensor and its attributes could be the temperature value, geographical location, and operational status of the sensor.

Orion Context Broker is designed to work with high-frequency real-time data, ensuring that context information is always up-to-date and available to applications that need it. It uses a scalable and distributed architecture to handle large volumes of data and ensure high performance even in high data intensity scenarios.

One of the key features of Orion Context Broker is its ability to publish and subscribe to real-time context changes. Applications can register to receive notifications when data in the system changes, allowing them to react instantly to significant events. For example, an air quality monitoring application could be alerted when pollutant levels exceed certain limits.

Orion Context Broker also supports complex queries to retrieve context information based on specific criteria. Applications can query the system to obtain data relevant to their needs, filter the results, and aggregate them for more advanced analysis. This flexibility allows applications to dynamically adapt to changes in context and provide detailed and personalized information to end users.

Another important feature of Orion Context Broker is its ability to manage data access rights and privacy controls. Applications can specify who can access the data and how it can be used, ensuring compliance with data protection regulations and the security of sensitive information. This is particularly important in sensitive scenarios such as healthcare and public safety, where protecting personal data and ensuring confidentiality is crucial.

Orion Context Broker is designed to be highly interoperable and compatible with a wide range of industry technologies and standards. It supports standard protocols like MQTT, CoAP, and HTTP for communication with

IoT devices and external applications. Additionally, it is interoperable with other components of the FIWARE platform and can be easily integrated with existing systems thanks to its modular architecture and well-documented APIs.

FIWARE Orion Context Broker is a powerful and flexible tool for managing real-time context in intelligent applications. With its ability to handle large volumes of data, provide up-to-date information, and respond instantly to events, it is an essential component for the development of innovative and scalable solutions based on real-time data. With its interoperability, scalability, and security, Orion Context Broker provides organizations with a solid foundation for building intelligent and responsive applications that enhance efficiency, security, and quality of life.

5.FIWARE NGSI

FIWARE NGSI (Next Generation Service Interface) is an open and public standard developed by the FIWARE Foundation to manage information within IoT and smart city platforms. This standard defines a common data model and an application programming interface for accessing and manipulating information in an interoperable way.

The basic data model of NGSI consists of entities and attributes. An entity represents an object in the real world, such as a sensor, a lamp, or a person. Each entity has one or more attributes that describe its properties, such as the temperature measured by the sensor or the status of the lamp. Entities and attributes are identified by a unique type and identifier.

The basic operations offered by the NGSI interface include creating, reading, updating, and deleting entities and attributes. Additionally, it is possible to query entities based on specific filters and conditions.

An example of how NGSI works is as follows:

Imagine a system for monitoring air quality in a city, with various sensors distributed in different locations. Each sensor is represented by an entity with attributes such as air quality, temperature, and geographic location.

To add a new sensor to the system, we can send a request to create an entity like this:

POST /v2/entities

```json
{
  "id": "sensor_1",
  "type": "AirQualitySensor",
  "location": {
    "type": "Point",
    "coordinates": [45.12345, 9.54321]
  },
  "airQuality": {
    "value": 25,
    "type": "Number"
  },
  "temperature": {
    "value": 20,
    "type": "Number"
  }
}
```

In this example, we are creating a new air quality sensor with ID "sensor_1", located at the specified geographic coordinates, and with initial air quality and temperature values. Once the entity has been created in the system, we can read, update, or delete its attributes and query available sensors.

For example, we can query to get all air quality sensors with a temperature above 25 degrees:

GET /v2/entities?
type=AirQualitySensor&q=temperature>25

This will return a list of sensor entities that meet the specified search criteria.

Furthermore, NGSI supports real-time event-based notifications. For instance, we can configure the system to send a notification whenever a sensor's air quality exceeds a certain threshold:

POST /v2/subscriptions

```json
{
  "description": "Notify when air quality exceeds threshold",
  "subject": {
    "entities": [
      {
        "idPattern": "sensor_*",
        "type": "AirQualitySensor"
      }
    ],
    "condition": {
      "attrs": ["airQuality"],
      "expression": {
        "q": "airQuality>30"
```

```
      }

    }

  },

  "notification": {

    "http": {

      "url": "http://example.com/notify"

    }

  }

}
```

This subscription activates the system to send a notification to the specified URL whenever a sensor's air quality exceeds the threshold value of 30.

FIWARE NGSI is a powerful and flexible standard for managing information within IoT and smart city platforms. It defines a common data model and an application programming interface for accessing and manipulating information in an interoperable manner, enabling the creation of scalable and interconnected systems.

6. FIWARE Data Models

Within FIWARE, Data Models play a fundamental role as they provide a common structure for representing and managing data in a standardized way.

Data Models in FIWARE are defined using a data modeling specification called NGSI (Next Generation Service Interface), which allows for defining entities, attributes, and relationships coherently and interoperably. Each entity in a Data Model is represented by a JSON object that contains a series of attributes with associated values.

One of the most well-known examples of a Data Model in FIWARE is the Data Model for Smart Cities, which defines a series of entities and attributes to represent information related to a smart city. For example, the "Building" entity could contain attributes such as "name," "address," "building type," and "energy consumption."

Another example of a Data Model in FIWARE is the Data Model for sensor management, which defines a series of entities and attributes to represent information coming from sensors installed in an IoT environment. For example, the "Sensor" entity could contain attributes such as "sensor type," "location," "measured value," and "acquisition timestamp."

FIWARE Data Models are designed to be flexible and extensible, allowing developers to adapt them to their specific needs. Additionally, the platform provides tools for managing and validating Data Models, ensuring data consistency and interoperability within an ecosystem of applications.

Another important aspect of Data Models in FIWARE is the ability to define relationships between entities, allowing for effectively modeling complex interactions between different types of data. For example, a Data Model for traffic management could define a relationship between the "Vehicle" entity and the "Road" entity to represent traffic flow in a specific area.

FIWARE Data Models represent a key element for the development of intelligent and interconnected applications. Thanks to their flexibility and standardization, Data Models allow developers to efficiently model and manage a wide range of data, fostering innovation and the creation of advanced solutions for real-world challenges.

7.FIWARE Identity Manager

The FIWARE Identity Manager is an identity management solution that provides users with complete control over their personal data and permissions to access online resources and services securely and reliably. This platform is designed to ensure the privacy and security of user data, allowing them to effectively manage their personal information and authenticate access to digital platforms.

One of the key features of the FIWARE Identity Manager is its ability to allow users to easily register and authenticate their digital identities across different platforms and online services. This means that users can use the same login credentials to access different online services without having to create new accounts or provide personal information repeatedly.

For example, a user could register their identity on an e-commerce website using the FIWARE Identity Manager and later use the same credentials to access an online banking app without having to provide new personal information. This not only simplifies the access process for users but also ensures the security of their personal information, avoiding unauthorized disclosure of data.

Furthermore, the FIWARE Identity Manager offers online service providers the ability to securely manage user permissions and allow them to control which information can be shared with third parties. For instance, a user may choose to share their contact information with a social networking app but not allow access to their financial data.

This permission management feature allows users to retain complete control over their personal information and decide who can access it and for how long. Additionally, the FIWARE Identity Manager utilizes advanced security protocols, such as OAuth and OpenID Connect, to ensure the protection of user data during the authentication and authorization process.

Another key feature of the FIWARE Identity Manager is its ability to support authenticated digital identity through multiple factors, such as passwords, tokens, and biometrics. This ensures a higher level of security for users, as they can choose the authentication method that best suits their level of risk and personal preferences.

Additionally, the FIWARE Identity Manager offers an intuitive and user-friendly interface that allows users to easily manage their digital identities, access permissions, and authorizations quickly and securely. Users can view and modify their personal information, revoke permissions granted to third parties, and control access to their data at any time and from any device.

The FIWARE Identity Manager is an advanced and secure solution for managing digital identities that ensures the security, privacy, and control of users over their personal information and access to online services. With advanced features, robust security protocols, and an intuitive user interface, this platform is ideal for users and online service providers seeking an effective and reliable solution for managing digital identities.

8.FIWARE Generic Enablers

FIWARE (Future Internet Ware) is an open-source platform designed to facilitate the development of intelligent and interconnected applications in the Internet of Things (IoT), Smart Cities, and Industry 4.0. One of the key elements of FIWARE is the Generic Enablers (GEs), software components that provide key functionalities and basic services for creating innovative applications.

FIWARE Generic Enablers are divided into two main categories: Core Enablers and Add-On Enablers. Core Enablers provide essential functionalities for data and resource management, security, and interoperability among different devices and systems. Add-On Enablers, on the other hand, offer specialized functionalities and specific services for certain sectors or applications.

One of the most important Core Enablers of

FIWARE is the Orion Context Broker, a data management system that allows real-time management of contextualized information from various sources and devices. This GE enables the dynamic creation and modification of information contexts and notification of events based on specific conditions.

Another relevant Core Enabler is Cosmos, a big data storage and analysis system that allows efficient and scalable storage and analysis of large volumes of data. With Cosmos, complex queries can be executed on huge datasets and real-time results can be obtained.

Among FIWARE's Add-On Enablers are specialized GEs for specific sectors, such as SmartSDK for developing applications for Smart Cities, or STEVE for managing and analyzing data from IoT sensors. These GEs provide dedicated tools and services to address the challenges and specific needs of certain sectors or application contexts.

Another example of a Generic Enabler is WireCloud, a framework for creating customized mashups and dashboards that integrates and visualizes data from various sources in a single intuitive and customizable interface. With WireCloud, innovative and tailored solutions can be created for the specific needs of users and organizations.

Another category of interesting GEs are those related to security, such as Keyrock for user access and identity management, and PEP Proxy for access control to resources and protection of sensitive data. These GEs are crucial for ensuring the security and privacy of information exchanged and managed within the FIWARE platform.

FIWARE Generic Enablers are designed to be easily integrable and configurable into any existing application or system, allowing developers to create innovative and scalable solutions quickly and efficiently. Thanks to the flexibility and versatility of FIWARE GEs, intelligent and interconnected applications can be created in various sectors such as agriculture, energy, mobility, and healthcare.

FIWARE Generic Enablers are the beating heart of the platform, offering essential functionalities and services for the development of advanced and intelligent applications. With a wide range of GEs available, the challenges and opportunities of the digital world can be addressed in an innovative and sustainable way.

9. FIWARE Context Data

The FIWARE Context Data is a key concept within the FIWARE ecosystem, an open-source platform that provides a set of tools and components for the development and management of smart and connected applications. This concept refers to the representation of contextual data within the development environment, allowing developers to access, manage, and use relevant information for their applications efficiently and flexibly.

FIWARE Context Data is based on three fundamental elements: entities, attributes, and values. Entities represent real-world objects that are monitored or controlled within the application's context. Attributes are the characteristics or parameters that define the entities and describe their state or properties. Finally, values are the data representing the values of the attributes of the entities at a given moment.

A concrete example of how FIWARE Context Data can be used is in the smart city sector. Imagine wanting to create an application that provides real-time traffic information within a city. Using FIWARE Context Data, we could define entities corresponding to vehicles, traffic sensors, and roads, attributes such as speed, position, and traffic status, and values like traffic sensor data that are continuously updated.

In this scenario, FIWARE Context Data allows us to structurally and organizedly represent traffic information, facilitating access and data management by the application. Furthermore, the flexible data model of FIWARE Context Data allows for easy adaptation and modification of data representation according to application needs, ensuring greater scalability and customization.

In addition to contextual data representation,

FIWARE Context Data also offers advanced features for data management and processing, such as real-time data querying, event notification, and business rule management. These features enable developers to implement complex business logic and create intelligent and responsive applications that dynamically respond to changes in the context.

FIWARE Context Data represents a key element for the development of smart and connected applications within the FIWARE ecosystem. Thanks to its ability to represent contextual data efficiently and flexibly, it facilitates the creation of innovative and customized solutions for a wide range of sectors, from the Internet of Things to smart cities, from smart agriculture to digital health.

10. The FIWARE IoT

The FIWARE IoT Agent is a fundamental tool for managing and integrating IoT devices within an infrastructure based on FIWARE. This software component allows interfacing with heterogeneous devices, acquiring real-time data, and sending it to a FIWARE data context for processing and analysis.

The FIWARE IoT Agent is based on a standardized communication scheme called NGSI (Next Generation Service Interface), which defines how devices and applications should exchange information and commands in an interoperable manner. This scheme provides a set of APIs and interfaces for device and data management, ensuring greater flexibility and scalability in implementing IoT solutions.

One of the main advantages of the FIWARE IoT Agent is its ability to manage a large number of heterogeneous devices, supporting various communication protocols such as MQTT, CoAP, HTTP, and others. Thanks to this flexibility, it is possible to easily integrate new devices into the existing infrastructure without having to adhere to strict constraints on the type of device or protocol used.

A practical example of using the FIWARE IoT Agent could involve monitoring an industrial plant composed of various sensors and actuators. Suppose we have a temperature sensor that sends real-time data via the MQTT protocol. The FIWARE IoT Agent can be configured to receive this data, transform it into a format compatible with the FIWARE data context, and send it to the Broker Context Manager for processing.

In this scenario, the FIWARE IoT Agent acts as an intermediary between the sensor and the FIWARE platform, handling incoming and outgoing communication in a transparent and reliable manner. Thanks to this architecture based on open standards and flexibility, it is possible to easily integrate new devices and deploy the IoT solution at scale without compatibility issues or performance limitations.

Another advantage of the FIWARE IoT Agent is its ability to implement advanced security policies to protect sensitive data and ensure user privacy. By configuring access and permissions, it is possible to ensure that only authorized users can access data and control devices, reducing the risk of unauthorized access or privacy breaches.

Furthermore, the FIWARE IoT Agent provides tools to monitor device performance and detect any anomalies or operational issues in real time. Thanks to telemetry and configurable alerts, it is possible to promptly respond to any critical situation and ensure the proper functioning of the IoT infrastructure.

Ultimately, the FIWARE IoT Agent is designed to be extendable and customizable according to the specific needs of each IoT application. With its modular architecture and detailed documentation, it is possible to integrate new features and customize the software's behavior based on the project's requirements.

The FIWARE IoT Agent represents a comprehensive and scalable solution for managing and integrating IoT devices within a FIWARE-based infrastructure. With its flexibility, security, and ability to handle a large number of heterogeneous devices, this software component offers a wide range of possibilities for the development of advanced and high-performance IoT solutions.

11. FIWARE Security

FIWARE Security is an open-source platform that provides a range of tools and services to ensure the security of applications developed using FIWARE technologies. Security is a fundamental aspect of any computer system, especially when it comes to managing sensitive or critical data. FIWARE Security offers a set of functionalities that allow developers to protect their applications from external threats and ensure the confidentiality, integrity, and availability of data.

One central aspect of FIWARE Security is identity and access management. This allows defining who can access the system resources and with what rights. For example, an application developed on FIWARE may require users to authenticate using valid credentials before accessing its features. FIWARE Security offers tools to securely manage user credentials, preventing them from being compromised by cyber attacks.

Another important aspect of security in FIWARE is the protection of data in transit and at rest. This means that information exchanged between different components of the application must be encrypted to prevent interception by unauthorized third parties. Additionally, data stored on servers must be protected from unauthorized access using encryption mechanisms and access control.

FIWARE Security also provides advanced communication security features, such as SSL/TLS certificate management and protection against Man-in-the-Middle attacks. This ensures that the information exchanged between different components of the application remains confidential and intact, avoiding compromise by malicious agents.

A practical example of how FIWARE Security can be used to protect applications is an online payment application. In this case,

FIWARE Security could be used to securely manage the identities of users making online transactions, ensuring that only authorized users can make payments and access sensitive financial information. Additionally, FIWARE Security could be used to encrypt transaction data during transmission over the network, protecting them from Man-in-the-Middle attacks that could compromise transaction security.

Furthermore, FIWARE Security offers tools for detecting and preventing cyber attacks, such as security event management and system log management. This allows developers to constantly monitor the system and identify any anomalies or suspicious behavior that may indicate an ongoing attack. This way, security threats can be promptly mitigated and applications protected from potential damage.

Lastly, FIWARE Security also supports compliance with regulations on personal data protection, such as GDPR. This means that applications developed on FIWARE can be designed to comply with privacy and data protection regulations, ensuring that users' personal information is treated securely and in accordance with the law.

FIWARE Security offers a range of advanced features to protect applications developed on FIWARE from external threats and ensure the security of exchanged and stored information. With its identity management, encryption, attack detection, and regulatory compliance features, FIWARE Security provides a solid foundation for building secure and GDPR-compliant applications.

12. FIWARE Business API Ecosystem

FIWARE Security is an open-source platform that provides a set of tools and services to ensure the security of applications developed using FIWARE technologies. Security is a fundamental aspect of any computer system, especially when it comes to handling sensitive or critical data. FIWARE Security offers a set of features that allow developers to protect their applications from external threats and ensure the confidentiality, integrity, and availability of data.

One of the central aspects of FIWARE Security is identity and access management. This allows defining who can access the resources of the system and with what rights. For example, an application developed on FIWARE may require users to authenticate using valid credentials before accessing its features. FIWARE Security offers tools to securely manage user credentials, preventing them from being compromised by cyber-attacks.

Another important aspect of security in FIWARE is the protection of data in transit and at rest. This means that information exchanged between the different components of the application must be encrypted to prevent interception by unauthorized third parties. Additionally, data stored on servers must be protected from unauthorized access using encryption mechanisms and access controls.

FIWARE Security also offers advanced features for communication security, such as SSL/TLS certificate management and protection against Man-in-the-Middle attacks. This way, information exchanged between different components of the application remains confidential and intact, preventing compromise by malicious actors.

A practical example of how FIWARE

Security can be used to protect applications is in an online payment application. In this case, FIWARE Security could be used to securely manage the identities of users making online transactions, ensuring that only authorized users can make payments and access sensitive financial information. Furthermore, FIWARE Security could be used to encrypt transaction data during transmission over the network, protecting them from Man-in-the-Middle attacks that could compromise transaction security.

Additionally, FIWARE Security offers tools for detecting and preventing cyber-attacks, such as security event management and system logs. This allows developers to constantly monitor the system and identify any anomalies or suspicious behavior that may indicate an ongoing attack. This way, security threats can be promptly mitigated to protect applications from potential harm.

Finally, FIWARE Security also supports

compliance with data protection regulations, such as the GDPR. This means that applications developed on FIWARE can be designed to adhere to privacy and data protection regulations, ensuring that users' personal information is treated securely and in compliance with the law.

FIWARE Security offers a range of advanced features to protect applications developed on FIWARE from external threats and ensure the security of exchanged and stored information. With its identity management, encryption, attack detection, and regulatory compliance features, FIWARE Security represents a solid foundation for building secure and compliant applications that adhere to data protection regulations.

13. FIWARE Marketplace

The FIWARE Marketplace is an online platform that allows developers to find, test, and use services and software components based on FIWARE technologies. This marketplace offers a wide range of resources and tools that can be used to develop and implement innovative solutions in various sectors such as smart cities, smart agriculture, urban mobility, and more.

One of the main advantages of the FIWARE Marketplace is the ability to access a large variety of ready-to-use services and components, which allows developers to save time and resources in the development phase of their applications. For example, an application dedicated to smart energy management could utilize services such as real-time weather data, energy consumption data, lighting and heating management systems, all available on the FIWARE Marketplace.

Furthermore, the FIWARE Marketplace offers the option to test services for free before purchasing them, allowing developers to evaluate the quality and functionalities of each component before integrating it into their application. This approach helps reduce risks and enhance the quality of the final product.

Another important aspect of the FIWARE Marketplace is the presence of an active and collaborative community, composed of experts, developers, and users who share knowledge, experiences, and best practices on the use of FIWARE technologies. Thanks to this community, developers can receive technical support, consultations, and tips to improve their solutions and overcome any obstacles during the development process.

In terms of security and privacy, the FIWARE Marketplace guarantees the protection of sensitive data of users and companies using the services and components available on the platform. All service providers are required to comply with European regulations on personal data protection and adopt best practices to ensure the security of transmitted and stored information.

Lastly, the FIWARE Marketplace offers a wide range of cross-cutting solutions that can be used in various sectors and contexts, allowing developers to create innovative applications and services that meet the specific needs of their customers. For example, an application for monitoring air quality could utilize services such as environmental sensors, meteorological data, air pollution prediction models, and much more.

The FIWARE Marketplace is a crucial resource for developers looking to create advanced solutions based on FIWARE technologies, offering a wide range of ready-to-use services and components, support from the community, and guarantees in terms of data security and privacy. Through this platform, it is possible to accelerate the development process, reduce costs, and increase efficiency in creating innovative and scalable solutions for various sectors of the Internet of Things (IoT).

14. FIWARE IoT Stack

FIWARE is an open-source platform that provides a stack of technologies for IoT, aimed at facilitating the development of intelligent and innovative applications. The FIWARE IoT Stack includes various components that allow for managing data from connected devices in real-time and using them to create advanced services and solutions.

One of the main components of the FIWARE IoT Stack is Orion Context Broker, a data management system that allows for storing and querying information about the status of connected devices and taking actions based on specific events. For example, if a sensor detects a fire alarm, Orion Context Broker can automatically trigger an evacuation system.

Another fundamental component is Cygnus, a persistence agent that transforms unstructured data from devices into structured format and stores it in a database for analysis and visualization. For example, Cygnus can collect data from sensors in a production plant and store it in a database to monitor performance and identify any issues.

The FIWARE IoT Stack also includes components for user authentication and authorization, such as Keyrock, which manages access to resources and APIs securely and controlled. This ensures that only authorized users can access sensitive data from connected devices.

Another important component is Wilma, a middleware for communication between IoT devices and the FIWARE platform. Wilma efficiently manages data transmission from sensors to servers and vice versa, ensuring reliable and secure communication between connected devices and the platform.

Lastly, the FIWARE IoT Stack also includes WireCloud, a visual development environment that allows for quickly and easily creating customized dashboards to monitor data from connected devices and creating interactive widgets to display real-time information. For example, a dashboard could be created to monitor the energy consumption of a building or the status of an automatic irrigation system.

The FIWARE IoT Stack provides a comprehensive and integrated set of technologies for developing advanced and intelligent IoT solutions. With its flexible and scalable components, it is possible to quickly and easily create innovative applications that leverage data from connected devices to improve people's lives and optimize business processes.

15. FIWARE Smart Cities

FIWARE is an open-source platform that allows for the development and management of IoT and Smart Cities solutions in an efficient and scalable manner. This technology offers a range of tools and software components that can be used to create intelligent and connected applications to improve the quality of life in urban areas.

One of the main goals of FIWARE Smart Cities is to provide citizens with smart and sustainable services and infrastructure through the use of advanced and innovative technologies. In this context, the FIWARE platform serves as a fundamental tool for the realization of Smart Cities, enabling the integration and management of a wide range of data from sensors, devices, and systems distributed throughout the city.

An example of how FIWARE can be used to

improve energy efficiency in a Smart City is the implementation of a system for monitoring and controlling the energy consumption of buildings. By using sensors and intelligent devices installed in buildings, it is possible to collect and analyze data related to energy consumption and the energy performance of properties.

Thanks to the FIWARE platform, it is possible to integrate and display this information in real-time, allowing administrators to make targeted interventions to optimize energy usage and reduce costs. For example, it is possible to automatically adjust the temperature of buildings based on external weather conditions, schedule the shutdown of unnecessary devices during off-peak hours, and monitor the overall energy consumption of the facilities.

Another sector in which FIWARE can be successfully employed is that of intelligent urban mobility. Through the use of sensors, cameras, and connected infrastructure, it is possible to monitor and manage city traffic in real-time, improving road safety and optimizing the flows of vehicles and pedestrians.

For example, using the FIWARE platform, it is possible to create an intelligent traffic management system that automatically detects road incidents, adjusts traffic lights based on traffic conditions, and provides real-time updates on road developments to citizens through mobile applications and information panels. In this way, it is possible to reduce travel times, improve air quality, and promote a more sustainable use of transportation.

16. FIWARE Open Data

FIWARE Open Data is a platform developed to facilitate access and sharing of open and interoperable data. Thanks to its modular and scalable architecture, FIWARE Open Data allows users to easily access a wide variety of data from different sources and integrate them into innovative applications and services.

One of the key features of FIWARE Open Data is its ability to efficiently handle large volumes of data. With the support of advanced technologies such as cloud computing and Big Data, FIWARE Open Data can process and analyze huge amounts of data in real-time, enabling users to obtain valuable and relevant information in a timely manner.

Furthermore, FIWARE Open Data offers a range of tools and services to facilitate data visualization and analysis. Users can use customizable dashboards and advanced analytics tools to explore and interpret data in meaningful and informative ways. This allows them to identify trends, spot correlations, and make informed decisions based on the available data.

Another advantage of FIWARE Open Data is its ability to promote collaboration and sharing among various actors in the public and private sectors. Thanks to its open and interoperable nature, FIWARE Open Data enables users to easily share their data and collaborate with others to develop new solutions and services based on the available data.

One example of how FIWARE Open Data can be used is in the public transportation sector. Local authorities can use the platform to share data related to public transport schedules, routes, and real-time traffic conditions. Developers can then use this data to create navigation and trip planning applications that help citizens move efficiently and sustainably within the city.

Another example relates to the healthcare sector. Healthcare service providers can use FIWARE Open Data to share information about patients and healthcare performance, allowing healthcare professionals to access crucial data in real-time and improve the quality and efficiency of care provided to patients.

FIWARE Open Data is a powerful and versatile platform that offers users the opportunity to access and share open data in innovative and meaningful ways. With its advanced architecture and sophisticated features, FIWARE Open Data can support a wide range of applications and services, enabling users to fully harness the potential of open data to create value and promote innovation in various sectors.

17. FIWARE Cloud Hosting

FIWARE is an open-source, cloud-based standard platform that offers a wide range of services for the development and execution of intelligent and innovative applications. FIWARE Cloud Hosting is one of the services offered by FIWARE that allows users to easily and efficiently create, manage, and deploy their infrastructure and applications on the cloud.

FIWARE Cloud Hosting offers a range of features and benefits that make it an ideal choice for businesses of all sizes looking to leverage the power of cloud computing. Some of the key advantages include flexibility in resource allocation and management, scalability to adapt to evolving business needs, data security ensured by robust protection mechanisms, and support for a wide range of technologies and frameworks.

To use FIWARE Cloud Hosting, users can access the platform through an intuitive and user-friendly web interface that allows them to easily create and configure their virtual machines, networks, and cloud services. With extensive documentation and an active FIWARE community, users can easily find guides, tutorials, and support to make the most of all the platform's features.

A concrete example of using FIWARE Cloud Hosting could involve a company wanting to develop and deploy an artificial intelligence application for real-time data analysis. By using FIWARE Cloud Hosting, the company could easily create a series of virtual machines and cloud services to manage data processing, AI model training, and application deployment to end users.

With the flexibility and scalability of FIWARE Cloud Hosting, the company could dynamically increase or decrease allocated resources based on workload demands, ensuring optimal performance and cost-effectiveness. Data security would be ensured by advanced encryption and access control mechanisms, complying with privacy regulations and safeguarding sensitive data.

Furthermore, with support for a wide range of technologies and frameworks, the company could easily integrate its AI applications with other existing services and systems such as databases, authentication services, and performance monitoring. This would enable the company to create comprehensive and cutting-edge solutions that fully meet the needs of its clients and users.

FIWARE Cloud Hosting is a comprehensive and high-performance solution for developing, managing, and deploying cloud infrastructure and applications. With its advanced features, reliability, and flexibility, FIWARE Cloud Hosting is the ideal choice for businesses looking to maximize the benefits of cloud computing and accelerate their success in the digital world.

18.Advantages and disadvantages of FIWARE

FIWARE is an open-source platform that provides a range of tools and software components for the development of intelligent and innovative applications based on the Internet of Things (IoT), big data, and artificial intelligence. It has quickly gained popularity among developers and businesses for its flexibility, scalability, and interoperability. However, like any technology, it has advantages and disadvantages that are important to consider before adopting it to develop your own solutions.

Advantages of FIWARE:

1. Interoperability and open standards: FIWARE is based on open standards and common protocols to ensure interoperability between different devices and systems. This means that new sensors, actuators, and software platforms can be easily integrated without radically changing the entire architecture.

2. Scalability and flexibility: FIWARE is designed to handle large amounts of data from various sources and devices. Its distributed architecture allows for efficient horizontal and vertical scaling to meet the needs of projects of any size.

3. Modularity and reusable components: FIWARE offers a wide range of software components and tools that can be easily integrated into your solutions. This reduces development times and costs, as well as

ensuring greater consistency and cohesion in the implementation of functionalities.

4. Security and access control: FIWARE includes advanced features to ensure the security of applications and sensitive data. Access permissions can be managed granularly, and suspicious activities can be monitored in real-time to prevent potential security threats.

5. Community support and documentation: FIWARE is supported by a large community of developers, experts, and partners who provide assistance and resources to solve any issues during application development. Detailed documentation and tutorials simplify learning and using the platform.

Disadvantages of FIWARE:

1. Complexity of the architecture: FIWARE is a complex platform that requires a learning curve to fully understand its capabilities and functionalities. Developers and users may find it difficult to navigate through the various available components and modules, especially if they do not have a deep knowledge of the architecture.

2. Implementation and maintenance costs: Although FIWARE is open-source, implementing and maintaining a solution based on this platform can require significant resources in terms of time, money, and specialized personnel. It is important to carefully evaluate the costs and benefits before deciding to adopt FIWARE for a specific project.

3. Dependence on external resources: Since FIWARE is based on a community of developers and external partners, some key components or services may be subject to changes or discontinuity over time. This could lead to compatibility or interoperability issues with previous versions of your solutions.

4. Performance limitations in complex scenarios: In some cases, FIWARE may show limitations in performance when handling large volumes of data or in very complex operational scenarios. It is crucial to carefully assess the performance and scalability requirements of your project before choosing FIWARE as a development platform.

5. Limited support for some emerging technologies: Despite the wide range of components and tools available, FIWARE may not support some emerging or cutting-edge technologies that may be relevant to specific industries or use cases. It is important to verify the compatibility and availability of alternative solutions before adopting FIWARE for advanced or experimental projects.

FIWARE offers numerous advantages for the development of intelligent and innovative applications, but it also has some disadvantages that must be taken into consideration. Carefully evaluating the requirements of your project, the available resources, and potential risks is essential to ensure the success of implementing FIWARE and maximize the benefits that this platform can offer.

Index